The Course Key: A 16 Week Guided Study Tool

KATIE WILLIAMS
EDUCATOR & CREATOR

Copyright © 2019 by Katie Williams

All rights reserved. This journal or any portion thereof may not be reproduced or used in any manner whatsoever without the express written permission of the creator. This work is sold with the understanding that the creator will not be held responsible for the results accrued from using this book or for any grade earned in a course. This is simply an organizational tool, outcomes are based on the motivation of the student using it.

First Printing: 2019
ISBN 978-1-7333249-0-8
Williams Originals LLC
3013 Broadway Ave, Ste 8 #145
Yankton, SD, 57078

www.WilliamsOriginals.com

Ordering Information:
Special discounts are available on quantity purchases by corporations, associations, educators, and others. For details, contact the creator at the above listed address.

U.S. trade bookstores and wholesalers please contact:
Attn: Katie Williams
Williams Originals LLC
Tel: 701-541-7250
Email: williamsoriginals@gmail.com

Dedication

To my senior dental hygiene students:
Relax.
Take a breath.
Keep going.

May will be here in no time.

Table Of Contents

Course Info
Semester Outline & Calendar
Study Tips

Week 1
Week 2
Week 3
Week 4
Week 5
Week 6
Week 7
Week 8

MIDTERM

Week 9
Week 10
Week 11
Week 12
Week 13
Week 14
Week 15
Week 16

Exam 1
Exam 2
Exam 3
Exam 4
Final Exam

COURSE *info*

Instructor

#:

Schedule:

Email:

Schedule

Days:

Times:

Tutorng Options:

Resources

Books:

Online Resources:

Special Notes

THE COURSE KEY

Semester at a Glance
FIRST 8 WEEK COURSE OUTLINE
IMPORTANT DATES

WEEK 1

- [ ] Modules & Required Reading:

- [ ] Due Dates/Exams:

WEEK 2

- [ ] Modules & Required Reading:

- [ ] Due Dates/Exams:

WEEK 3

- [ ] Modules & Required Reading:

- [ ] Due Dates/Exams:

WEEK 4

- [ ] Modules & Required Reading:

- [ ] Due Dates/Exams:

WEEK 5

- [ ] Modules & Required Reading:

- [ ] Due Dates/Exams:

WEEK 6

- [ ] Modules & Required Reading:

- [ ] Due Dates/Exams:

WEEK 7

- [ ] Modules & Required Reading:

- [ ] Due Dates/Exams:

WEEK 8

- [ ] Modules & Required Reading:

- [ ] Due Dates/Exams:

Semester at a Glance
SECOND 8 WEEK COURSE OUTLINE
IMPORTANT DATES

WEEK 9

- [ ] Modules & Required Reading:

- [ ] Due Dates/Exams:

WEEK 10

- [ ] Modules & Required Reading:

- [ ] Due Dates/Exams:

WEEK 11

- [ ] Modules & Required Reading:

- [ ] Due Dates/Exams:

WEEK 12

- [ ] Modules & Required Reading:

- [ ] Due Dates/Exams:

WEEK 13

- [ ] Modules & Required Reading:

- [ ] Due Dates/Exams:

WEEK 14

- [ ] Modules & Required Reading:

- [ ] Due Dates/Exams:

WEEK 15

- [ ] Modules & Required Reading:

- [ ] Due Dates/Exams:

WEEK 16

- [ ] Modules & Required Reading:

- [ ] Due Dates/Exams:

Study Tips

A PERSONAL NOTE FROM ME:

Don't attempt to take on study habits you know you will not follow, but keep in mind you can't grow unless you challenge yourself. Here are some tried and true study habits I strongly encourage my students to keep. When they do these things, the results are positive and lasting.

1. No laptops/phones during lecture. Spare me the "technology" excuse. I've had students brag to me they planned their weddings on Pinterest in their pre-reqs... enough said.
2. Take required reading seriously. Take notes while preparing and have at least 2 questions ready for lecture. If they aren't answered during lecture, make sure to ask. Chances are, if you have the questions so does someone else.
3. Use the time before and after class wisely. It only takes about 5 minutes to clear your mind before class. Use the Brain Dump areas to do this. Also take time to reflect after lectures and tests. Immediately write down things you need to look up while they are fresh in your mind. It will remind you later what you need to study. There's no sense studying things you already have a good grasp on. Prioritizing difficult topics will make studying for your tests much more efficient!

THE COURSE KEY

Week 1

WHAT'S INSIDE:
1 WEEK PREP PAGE
3 LECTURE NOTES
1 WEEKLY SUMMARY

THE COURSE KEY

Week 1 Prep Page

MODULES TO COVER:

☐ *Required Reading*

- Chapters / Sections / Pages:

☐ *Notes From Reading*

☐ *Questions for Lecture*

Lecture Notes

Date:

Take 5 -
A 5 minute Brain Dump will clear your mind and prepare you for maximum information overload. Doodle and list below!

Main Lecture Notes:

1:

2:

3:

4:

5:

Practical Application of Lecture Topics:

1:

2:

3:

Test Priority Topics

1:

2:

❓ Say What?
Use this space to write questions that may arise during lecture.

THE COURSE KEY

Lecture Notes

Date:

Take 5 -
A 5 minute Brain Dump will clear your mind and prepare you for maximum information overload. Doodle and list below!

? Say What?
Use this space to write questions that may arise during lecture.

Main Lecture Notes:

1:

2:

3:

4:

5:

Practical Application of Lecture Topics:

1:

2:

3:

Test Priority Topics

1:

2:

THE COURSE KEY

Lecture Notes

Date:

Take 5 -
A 5 minute Brain Dump will clear your mind and prepare you for maximum information overload. Doodle and list below!

Main Lecture Notes:

1:

2:

3:

4:

5:

Practical Application of Lecture Topics:

1:

2:

3:

Test Priority Topics

1:

2:

? Say What?
Use this space to write questions that may arise during lecture.

THE COURSE KEY

Week 1 Summary Page

☐ *Lecture 1 Topics to Revisit*

☐ *Lecture 2 Topics to Revisit*

☐ *Lecture 3 Topics to Revisit*

Week 2

WHAT'S INSIDE:
1 WEEK PREP PAGE
3 LECTURE NOTES
1 WEEKLY SUMMARY

THE COURSE KEY

Week 2 Prep Page

MODULES TO COVER:

☐ *Required Reading*

- Chapters / Sections / Pages:

☐ *Notes From Reading*

☐ *Questions for Lecture*

Lecture Notes

Date:

Take 5 -
A 5 minute Brain Dump will clear your mind and prepare you for maximum information overload. Doodle and list below!

Main Lecture Notes:

1:

2:

3:

4:

5:

Practical Application of Lecture Topics:

1:

2:

3:

Test Priority Topics

1:

2:

? Say What?
Use this space to write questions that may arise during lecture.

THE COURSE KEY

Lecture Notes

Date:

Take 5 -
A 5 minute Brain Dump will clear your mind and prepare you for maximum information overload. Doodle and list below!

Say What?
Use this space to write questions that may arise during lecture.

Main Lecture Notes:

1:

2:

3:

4:

5:

Practical Application of Lecture Topics:

1:

2:

3:

Test Priority Topics

1:

2:

THE COURSE KEY

Lecture Notes

Date:

Take 5 -
A 5 minute Brain Dump will clear your mind and prepare you for maximum information overload. Doodle and list below!

Main Lecture Notes:

1:

2:

3:

4:

5:

Practical Application of Lecture Topics:

1:

2:

3:

Test Priority Topics

1:

2:

? Say What?
Use this space to write questions that may arise during lecture.

THE COURSE KEY

Week 2 Summary Page

☐ *Lecture 1 Topics to Revisit*

☐ *Lecture 2 Topics to Revisit*

☐ *Lecture 3 Topics to Revisit*

Week 3

WHAT'S INSIDE:
1 WEEK PREP PAGE
3 LECTURE NOTES
1 WEEKLY SUMMARY

THE COURSE KEY

Week 3 Prep Page

MODULES TO COVER:

☐ *Required Reading*

- Chapters / Sections / Pages:

☐ *Notes From Reading*

☐ *Questions for Lecture*

The Course Key

Lecture Notes

Date:

Take 5 -
A 5 minute Brain Dump will clear your mind and prepare you for maximum information overload. Doodle and list below!

Main Lecture Notes:

1:

2:

3:

4:

5:

Practical Application of Lecture Topics:

1:

2:

3:

Test Priority Topics

1:

2:

? Say What?
Use this space to write questions that may arise during lecture.

THE COURSE KEY

Lecture Notes

Date:

Take 5 -
A 5 minute Brain Dump will clear your mind and prepare you for maximum information overload. Doodle and list below!

Say What?
Use this space to write questions that may arise during lecture.

Main Lecture Notes:

1:

2:

3:

4:

5:

Practical Application of Lecture Topics:

1:

2:

3:

Test Priority Topics

1:

2:

THE COURSE KEY

Lecture Notes

Date:

Take 5 -
A 5 minute Brain Dump will clear your mind and prepare you for maximum information overload. Doodle and list below!

Main Lecture Notes:

1:

2:

3:

4:

5:

Practical Application of Lecture Topics:

1:

2:

3:

Test Priority Topics

1:

2:

? Say What?
Use this space to write questions that may arise during lecture.

THE COURSE KEY

Week 3 Summary Page

- [ ] *Lecture 1 Topics to Revisit*

- [ ] *Lecture 2 Topics to Revisit*

- [ ] *Lecture 3 Topics to Revisit*

Week 4

WHAT'S INSIDE:
1 WEEK PREP PAGE
3 LECTURE NOTES
1 WEEKLY SUMMARY

THE COURSE KEY

Week 4 Prep Page

MODULES TO COVER:

☐ **Required Reading**

- Chapters / Sections / Pages:

☐ **Notes From Reading**

☐ **Questions for Lecture**

Lecture Notes

Date:

Take 5 -
A 5 minute Brain Dump will clear your mind and prepare you for maximum information overload. Doodle and list below!

❓ Say What?
Use this space to write questions that may arise during lecture.

Main Lecture Notes:

1:

2:

3:

4:

5:

Practical Application of Lecture Topics:

1:

2:

3:

Test Priority Topics

1:

2:

THE COURSE KEY

Lecture Notes

Date:

Take 5 -
A 5 minute Brain Dump will clear your mind and prepare you for maximum information overload. Doodle and list below!

Say What?
Use this space to write questions that may arise during lecture.

Main Lecture Notes:

1:

2:

3:

4:

5:

Practical Application of Lecture Topics:

1:

2:

3:

Test Priority Topics

1:

2:

THE COURSE KEY

Lecture Notes

Date:

Take 5 -
A 5 minute Brain Dump will clear your mind and prepare you for maximum information overload. Doodle and list below!

Main Lecture Notes:

1:

2:

3:

4:

5:

? Say What?
Use this space to write questions that may arise during lecture.

Practical Application of Lecture Topics:

1:

2:

3:

Test Priority Topics

1:

2:

THE COURSE KEY

Week 4 Summary Page

☐ *Lecture 1 Topics to Revisit*

☐ *Lecture 2 Topics to Revisit*

☐ *Lecture 3 Topics to Revisit*

Week 5

WHAT'S INSIDE:
1 WEEK PREP PAGE
3 LECTURE NOTES
1 WEEKLY SUMMARY

THE COURSE KEY

Week 5 Prep Page

MODULES TO COVER:

☐ *Required Reading*

- Chapters / Sections / Pages:

☐ *Notes From Reading*

☐ *Questions for Lecture*

Lecture Notes

Date:

Take 5 -
A 5 minute Brain Dump will clear your mind and prepare you for maximum information overload. Doodle and list below!

Main Lecture Notes:

1:

2:

3:

4:

5:

Practical Application of Lecture Topics:

1:

2:

3:

Test Priority Topics

1:

2:

? *Say What?*
Use this space to write questions that may arise during lecture.

THE COURSE KEY

Lecture Notes

Date:

Take 5 -
A 5 minute Brain Dump will clear your mind and prepare you for maximum information overload. Doodle and list below!

❓ Say What?
Use this space to write questions that may arise during lecture.

Main Lecture Notes:

1:

2:

3:

4:

5:

Practical Application of Lecture Topics:

1:

2:

3:

Test Priority Topics

1:

2:

THE COURSE KEY

Lecture Notes

Date:

Take 5 -
A 5 minute Brain Dump will clear your mind and prepare you for maximum information overload. Doodle and list below!

Main Lecture Notes:

1:

2:

3:

4:

5:

Practical Application of Lecture Topics:

1:

2:

3:

Test Priority Topics

1:

2:

? Say What?
Use this space to write questions that may arise during lecture.

THE COURSE KEY

Week 5 Summary Page

☐ *Lecture 1 Topics to Revisit*

☐ *Lecture 2 Topics to Revisit*

☐ *Lecture 3 Topics to Revisit*

The Course Key

Week 6

WHAT'S INSIDE:
1 WEEK PREP PAGE
3 LECTURE NOTES
1 WEEKLY SUMMARY

THE COURSE KEY

Week 6 Prep Page

MODULES TO COVER:

☐ **Required Reading**

- Chapters / Sections / Pages:

☐ **Notes From Reading**

☐ **Questions for Lecture**

Lecture Notes

Date:

Take 5 -
A 5 minute Brain Dump will clear your mind and prepare you for maximum information overload. Doodle and list below!

Main Lecture Notes:

1:

2:

3:

4:

5:

Practical Application of Lecture Topics:

1:

2:

3:

Test Priority Topics

1:

2:

? Say What?
Use this space to write questions that may arise during lecture.

THE COURSE KEY

Lecture Notes

Date:

Take 5 -
A 5 minute Brain Dump will clear your mind and prepare you for maximum information overload. Doodle and list below!

Say What?
Use this space to write questions that may arise during lecture.

Main Lecture Notes:

1:

2:

3:

4:

5:

Practical Application of Lecture Topics:

1:

2:

3:

Test Priority Topics

1:

2:

THE COURSE KEY

Lecture Notes

Date:

Take 5 -
A 5 minute Brain Dump will clear your mind and prepare you for maximum information overload. Doodle and list below!

Main Lecture Notes:

1:

2:

3:

4:

5:

Practical Application of Lecture Topics:

1:

2:

3:

Test Priority Topics

1:

2:

? Say What?
Use this space to write questions that may arise during lecture.

THE COURSE KEY

Week 6 Summary Page

- [ ] *Lecture 1 Topics to Revisit*

- [ ] *Lecture 2 Topics to Revisit*

- [ ] *Lecture 3 Topics to Revisit*

The Course Key

Week 7

WHAT'S INSIDE:
1 WEEK PREP PAGE
3 LECTURE NOTES
1 WEEKLY SUMMARY

THE COURSE KEY

Week 7 Prep Page

MODULES TO COVER:

Required Reading

- Chapters / Sections / Pages:

Notes From Reading

Questions for Lecture

Lecture Notes

Date:

Take 5 -
A 5 minute Brain Dump will clear your mind and prepare you for maximum information overload. Doodle and list below!

Main Lecture Notes:

1:

2:

3:

4:

5:

Practical Application of Lecture Topics:

1:

2:

3:

Test Priority Topics

1:

2:

? Say What?
Use this space to write questions that may arise during lecture.

THE COURSE KEY

Lecture Notes

Date:

Take 5 -
A 5 minute Brain Dump will clear your mind and prepare you for maximum information overload. Doodle and list below!

Main Lecture Notes:

1:

2:

3:

4:

5:

Practical Application of Lecture Topics:

1:

2:

3:

Test Priority Topics

1:

2:

? Say What?
Use this space to write questions that may arise during lecture.

THE COURSE KEY

Lecture Notes

Date:

Take 5 -
A 5 minute Brain Dump will clear your mind and prepare you for maximum information overload.
Doodle and list below!

Say What?
Use this space to write questions that may arise during lecture.

Main Lecture Notes:

1:

2:

3:

4:

5:

Practical Application of Lecture Topics:

1:

2:

3:

Test Priority Topics

1:

2:

THE COURSE KEY

Week 7 Summary Page

☐ *Lecture 1 Topics to Revisit*

☐ *Lecture 2 Topics to Revisit*

☐ *Lecture 3 Topics to Revisit*

Week 8

WHAT'S INSIDE:
1 WEEK PREP PAGE
3 LECTURE NOTES
1 WEEKLY SUMMARY

THE COURSE KEY

Week 8 Prep Page

MODULES TO COVER:

☐ *Required Reading*

- Chapters / Sections / Pages:

☐ *Notes From Reading*

☐ *Questions for Lecture*

The Course Key

Lecture Notes

Date:

Take 5 -
A 5 minute Brain Dump will clear your mind and prepare you for maximum information overload. Doodle and list below!

❓ Say What?
Use this space to write questions that may arise during lecture.

Main Lecture Notes:

1:

2:

3:

4:

5:

Practical Application of Lecture Topics:

1:

2:

3:

Test Priority Topics

1:

2:

THE COURSE KEY

Lecture Notes

Date:

Take 5 -
A 5 minute Brain Dump will clear your mind and prepare you for maximum information overload. Doodle and list below!

❓ Say What?

Use this space to write questions that may arise during lecture.

Main Lecture Notes:

1:

2:

3:

4:

5:

Practical Application of Lecture Topics:

1:

2:

3:

Test Priority Topics

1:

2:

THE COURSE KEY

Lecture Notes

Date:

Take 5 -
A 5 minute Brain Dump will clear your mind and prepare you for maximum information overload. Doodle and list below!

Main Lecture Notes:

1:

2:

3:

4:

5:

Practical Application of Lecture Topics:

1:

2:

3:

Test Priority Topics

1:

2:

Say What?
Use this space to write questions that may arise during lecture.

Week 8 Summary Page

- [ ] *Lecture 1 Topics to Revisit*

- [ ] *Lecture 2 Topics to Revisit*

- [ ] *Lecture 3 Topics to Revisit*

Midterm Review

THE COURSE KEY

Midterm Review

THE COURSE KEY

Week 9

WHAT'S INSIDE:
1 WEEK PREP PAGE
3 LECTURE NOTES
1 WEEKLY SUMMARY

THE COURSE KEY

Week 9 Prep Page

MODULES TO COVER:

☐ *Required Reading*

- Chapters / Sections / Pages:

☐ *Notes From Reading*

☐ *Questions for Lecture*

The Course Key

Lecture Notes

Date:

Take 5 -
A 5 minute Brain Dump will clear your mind and prepare you for maximum information overload. Doodle and list below!

Main Lecture Notes:

1:

2:

3:

4:

5:

Practical Application of Lecture Topics:

1:

2:

3:

Test Priority Topics

1:

2:

? Say What?
Use this space to write questions that may arise during lecture.

THE COURSE KEY

Lecture Notes

Date:

Take 5 -
A 5 minute Brain Dump will clear your mind and prepare you for maximum information overload. Doodle and list below!

Main Lecture Notes:

1:

2:

3:

4:

5:

Practical Application of Lecture Topics:

1:

2:

3:

Test Priority Topics

1:

2:

? Say What?
Use this space to write questions that may arise during lecture.

THE COURSE KEY

Lecture Notes

Date:

Take 5 -
A 5 minute Brain Dump will clear your mind and prepare you for maximum information overload. Doodle and list below!

Main Lecture Notes:

1:

2:

3:

4:

5:

? *Say What?*
Use this space to write questions that may arise during lecture.

Practical Application of Lecture Topics:

1:

2:

3:

Test Priority Topics

1:

2:

THE COURSE KEY

Week 9 Summary Page

☐ *Lecture 1 Topics to Revisit*

☐ *Lecture 2 Topics to Revisit*

☐ *Lecture 3 Topics to Revisit*

The Course Key

Week 10

WHAT'S INSIDE:
1 WEEK PREP PAGE
3 LECTURE NOTES
1 WEEKLY SUMMARY

THE COURSE KEY

Week 10 Prep Page

MODULES TO COVER:

☐ *Required Reading*

- Chapters / Sections / Pages:

☐ *Notes From Reading*

☐ *Questions for Lecture*

The Course Key

Lecture Notes

Date:

Take 5 -
A 5 minute Brain Dump will clear your mind and prepare you for maximum information overload. Doodle and list below!

Main Lecture Notes:

1:

2:

3:

4:

5:

Practical Application of Lecture Topics:

1:

2:

3:

Test Priority Topics

1:

2:

? Say What?
Use this space to write questions that may arise during lecture.

Lecture Notes

Date:

Take 5 -
A 5 minute Brain Dump will clear your mind and prepare you for maximum information overload. Doodle and list below!

Say What?
Use this space to write questions that may arise during lecture.

Main Lecture Notes:

1:

2:

3:

4:

5:

Practical Application of Lecture Topics:

1:

2:

3:

Test Priority Topics

1:

2:

THE COURSE KEY

Lecture Notes

Date:

Take 5 -
A 5 minute Brain Dump will clear your mind and prepare you for maximum information overload.
Doodle and list below!

❓ *Say What?*
Use this space to write questions that may arise during lecture.

Main Lecture Notes:

1:

2:

3:

4:

5:

Practical Application of Lecture Topics:

1:

2:

3:

Test Priority Topics

1:

2:

THE COURSE KEY

Week 10 Summary Page

- [ ] *Lecture 1 Topics to Revisit*

- [ ] *Lecture 2 Topics to Revisit*

- [ ] *Lecture 3 Topics to Revisit*

Week 11

WHAT'S INSIDE:
1 WEEK PREP PAGE
3 LECTURE NOTES
1 WEEKLY SUMMARY

THE COURSE KEY

Week 11 Prep Page

MODULES TO COVER:

☐ *Required Reading*

- Chapters / Sections / Pages:

☐ *Notes From Reading*

☐ *Questions for Lecture*

Lecture Notes

Date:

Take 5 -
A 5 minute Brain Dump will clear your mind and prepare you for maximum information overload. Doodle and list below!

? Say What?
Use this space to write questions that may arise during lecture.

Main Lecture Notes:

1:

2:

3:

4:

5:

Practical Application of Lecture Topics:

1:

2:

3:

Test Priority Topics

1:

2:

THE COURSE KEY

Lecture Notes

Date:

Take 5 -
A 5 minute Brain Dump will clear your mind and prepare you for maximum information overload. Doodle and list below!

Main Lecture Notes:

1:

2:

3:

4:

5:

Practical Application of Lecture Topics:

1:

2:

3:

Test Priority Topics

1:

2:

? Say What?
Use this space to write questions that may arise during lecture.

THE COURSE KEY

Lecture Notes

Date:

Take 5 -
A 5 minute Brain Dump will clear your mind and prepare you for maximum information overload. Doodle and list below!

Main Lecture Notes:

1:

2:

3:

4:

5:

Practical Application of Lecture Topics:

1:

2:

3:

Test Priority Topics

1:

2:

❓ Say What?
Use this space to write questions that may arise during lecture.

THE COURSE KEY

Week 11 Summary Page

- [ ] *Lecture 1 Topics to Revisit*

- [ ] *Lecture 2 Topics to Revisit*

- [ ] *Lecture 3 Topics to Revisit*

Week 12

WHAT'S INSIDE:
1 WEEK PREP PAGE
3 LECTURE NOTES
1 WEEKLY SUMMARY

THE COURSE KEY

Week 12 Prep Page

MODULES TO COVER:

☐ Required Reading

- Chapters / Sections / Pages:

☐ Notes From Reading

☐ Questions for Lecture

Lecture Notes

Date:

Take 5 -
A 5 minute Brain Dump will clear your mind and prepare you for maximum information overload. Doodle and list below!

Main Lecture Notes:

1:

2:

3:

4:

5:

Practical Application of Lecture Topics:

1:

2:

3:

Test Priority Topics

1:

2:

? Say What?
Use this space to write questions that may arise during lecture.

THE COURSE KEY

Lecture Notes

Date:

Take 5 -
A 5 minute Brain Dump will clear your mind and prepare you for maximum information overload. Doodle and list below!

Main Lecture Notes:

1:

2:

3:

4:

5:

Practical Application of Lecture Topics:

1:

2:

3:

Test Priority Topics

1:

2:

Say What?

Use this space to write questions that may arise during lecture.

THE COURSE KEY

Lecture Notes

Date:

Take 5 -
A 5 minute Brain Dump will clear your mind and prepare you for maximum information overload. Doodle and list below!

Main Lecture Notes:

1:

2:

3:

4:

5:

Practical Application of Lecture Topics:

1:

2:

3:

Test Priority Topics

1:

2:

? Say What?
Use this space to write questions that may arise during lecture.

THE COURSE KEY

Week 12 Summary Page

☐ *Lecture 1 Topics to Revisit*

☐ *Lecture 2 Topics to Revisit*

☐ *Lecture 3 Topics to Revisit*

The Course Key

Week 13

WHAT'S INSIDE:
1 WEEK PREP PAGE
3 LECTURE NOTES
1 WEEKLY SUMMARY

THE COURSE KEY

Week 13 Prep Page

MODULES TO COVER:

☐ *Required Reading*

- Chapters / Sections / Pages:

☐ *Notes From Reading*

☐ *Questions for Lecture*

Lecture Notes

Date:

Take 5 -
A 5 minute Brain Dump will clear your mind and prepare you for maximum information overload. Doodle and list below!

Main Lecture Notes:

1:

2:

3:

4:

5:

Practical Application of Lecture Topics:

1:

2:

3:

Test Priority Topics

1:

2:

? Say What?
Use this space to write questions that may arise during lecture.

THE COURSE KEY

Lecture Notes

Date:

Take 5 -
A 5 minute Brain Dump will clear your mind and prepare you for maximum information overload. Doodle and list below!

? Say What?
Use this space to write questions that may arise during lecture.

Main Lecture Notes:

1:

2:

3:

4:

5:

Practical Application of Lecture Topics:

1:

2:

3:

Test Priority Topics

1:

2:

THE COURSE KEY

Lecture Notes

Date:

Take 5 -
A 5 minute Brain Dump will clear your mind and prepare you for maximum information overload.
Doodle and list below!

Main Lecture Notes:

1:

2:

3:

4:

5:

Practical Application of Lecture Topics:

1:

2:

3:

Test Priority Topics

1:

2:

? *Say What?*
Use this space to write questions that may arise during lecture.

THE COURSE KEY

Week 13 Summary Page

☐ *Lecture 1 Topics to Revisit*

☐ *Lecture 2 Topics to Revisit*

☐ *Lecture 3 Topics to Revisit*

The Course Key

Week 14

WHAT'S INSIDE:
1 WEEK PREP PAGE
3 LECTURE NOTES
1 WEEKLY SUMMARY

THE COURSE KEY

Week 14 Prep Page

MODULES TO COVER:

☐ *Required Reading*

- Chapters / Sections / Pages:

☐ *Notes From Reading*

☐ *Questions for Lecture*

The Course Key

Lecture Notes

Date:

Take 5 -
A 5 minute Brain Dump will clear your mind and prepare you for maximum information overload. Doodle and list below!

? Say What?
Use this space to write questions that may arise during lecture.

Main Lecture Notes:

1:

2:

3:

4:

5:

Practical Application of Lecture Topics:

1:

2:

3:

Test Priority Topics

1:

2:

THE COURSE KEY

Lecture Notes

Date:

Take 5 -
A 5 minute Brain Dump will clear your mind and prepare you for maximum information overload. Doodle and list below!

Say What?
Use this space to write questions that may arise during lecture.

Main Lecture Notes:

1:

2:

3:

4:

5:

Practical Application of Lecture Topics:

1:

2:

3:

Test Priority Topics

1:

2:

THE COURSE KEY

Lecture Notes

Date:

Take 5 -
A 5 minute Brain Dump will clear your mind and prepare you for maximum information overload. Doodle and list below!

Main Lecture Notes:

1:

2:

3:

4:

5:

Practical Application of Lecture Topics:

1:

2:

3:

Test Priority Topics

1:

2:

❓ Say What?
Use this space to write questions that may arise during lecture.

THE COURSE KEY

Week 14 Summary Page

☐ *Lecture 1 Topics to Revisit*

☐ *Lecture 2 Topics to Revisit*

☐ *Lecture 3 Topics to Revisit*

Week 15

WHAT'S INSIDE:
1 WEEK PREP PAGE
3 LECTURE NOTES
1 WEEKLY SUMMARY

THE COURSE KEY

Week 15 Prep Page

MODULES TO COVER:

☐ Required Reading

- Chapters / Sections / Pages:

☐ Notes From Reading

☐ Questions for Lecture

Lecture Notes

Date:

Take 5 -
A 5 minute Brain Dump will clear your mind and prepare you for maximum information overload. Doodle and list below!

Main Lecture Notes:

1:

2:

3:

4:

5:

Practical Application of Lecture Topics:

1:

2:

3:

Test Priority Topics

1:

2:

? Say What?
Use this space to write questions that may arise during lecture.

THE COURSE KEY

Lecture Notes

Date:

Take 5 -
A 5 minute Brain Dump will clear your mind and prepare you for maximum information overload. Doodle and list below!

Main Lecture Notes:

1:

2:

3:

4:

5:

Practical Application of Lecture Topics:

1:

2:

3:

Test Priority Topics

1:

2:

? Say What?
Use this space to write questions that may arise during lecture.

THE COURSE KEY

Lecture Notes

Date:

Take 5 -
A 5 minute Brain Dump will clear your mind and prepare you for maximum information overload. Doodle and list below!

❓ *Say What?*
Use this space to write questions that may arise during lecture.

Main Lecture Notes:

1:

2:

3:

4:

5:

Practical Application of Lecture Topics:

1:

2:

3:

Test Priority Topics

1:

2:

THE COURSE KEY

Week 15 Summary Page

☐ *Lecture 1 Topics to Revisit*

☐ *Lecture 2 Topics to Revisit*

☐ *Lecture 3 Topics to Revisit*

Week 16

WHAT'S INSIDE:
1 WEEK PREP PAGE
3 LECTURE NOTES
1 WEEKLY SUMMARY

THE COURSE KEY

Week 16 Prep Page

MODULES TO COVER:

☐ *Required Reading*

- Chapters / Sections / Pages:

☐ *Notes From Reading*

☐ *Questions for Lecture*

The Course Key

Lecture Notes

Date:

Take 5 -
A 5 minute Brain Dump will clear your mind and prepare you for maximum information overload. Doodle and list below!

Main Lecture Notes:

1:

2:

3:

4:

5:

Practical Application of Lecture Topics:

1:

2:

3:

Test Priority Topics

1:

2:

❓ Say What?
Use this space to write questions that may arise during lecture.

THE COURSE KEY

Lecture Notes

Date:

Take 5 -
A 5 minute Brain Dump will clear your mind and prepare you for maximum information overload. Doodle and list below!

Main Lecture Notes:

1:

2:

3:

4:

5:

Practical Application of Lecture Topics:

1:

2:

3:

Test Priority Topics

1:

2:

? Say What?
Use this space to write questions that may arise during lecture.

THE COURSE KEY

Lecture Notes

Date:

Take 5 -
A 5 minute Brain Dump will clear your mind and prepare you for maximum information overload. Doodle and list below!

Main Lecture Notes:

1:

2:

3:

4:

5:

Practical Application of Lecture Topics:

1:

2:

3:

Test Priority Topics

1:

2:

❓ Say What?
Use this space to write questions that may arise during lecture.

THE COURSE KEY

Week 16 Summary Page

☐ *Lecture 1 Topics to Revisit*

☐ *Lecture 2 Topics to Revisit*

☐ *Lecture 3 Topics to Revisit*

Test Prep

WHAT'S INSIDE:
4 UNIT EXAM GUIDES
1 FINAL EXAM GUIDE

THE COURSE KEY

Unit Exam 1

REVIEW YOUR LECTURE NOTES, AND LIST THE TOPICS YOU NEED TO REVISIT HERE.
INCLUDE RELEVANT PAGE NUMBERS AND/OR POWERPOINT LOCATIONS

Topic:

Topic:

Topic:

The Course Key

Unit Exam 1

REVIEW YOUR LECTURE NOTES, AND LIST THE TOPICS YOU NEED TO REVISIT HERE.
INCLUDE RELEVANT PAGE NUMBERS AND/OR POWERPOINT LOCATIONS

Topic:

Topic:

Topic:

The Course Key

Unit Exam 1

REVIEW YOUR LECTURE NOTES, AND LIST THE TOPICS YOU NEED TO REVISIT HERE.
INCLUDE RELEVANT PAGE NUMBERS AND/OR POWERPOINT LOCATIONS

Topic:

Topic:

Topic:

The Course Key

Unit Exam 1

EXAM SUMMARY:

FILL OUT THIS WORKSHEET IMMEDIATELY AFTER

THE TEST TO HELP PREPARE FOR THE FINAL

> **Question Themes:**
> List below all of the major themes you were not prepared for and prioritize them for the final exam.

> **Question Types:**
> Recall all question types used and to what frequency. Reflect on what types you need to practice.

> **Successes:**
> Recall topics you had good understanding of and could easily answer. When studying for the final exam, briefly review these topics and move on!

The Course Key

Unit Exam 2

REVIEW YOUR LECTURE NOTES, AND LIST THE TOPICS YOU NEED TO REVISIT HERE.
INCLUDE RELEVANT PAGE NUMBERS AND/OR POWERPOINT LOCATIONS

Topic:

Topic:

Topic:

Unit Exam 2

REVIEW YOUR LECTURE NOTES, AND LIST THE TOPICS YOU NEED TO REVISIT HERE.
INCLUDE RELEVANT PAGE NUMBERS AND/OR POWERPOINT LOCATIONS

Topic:

Topic:

Topic:

Unit Exam 2

REVIEW YOUR LECTURE NOTES, AND LIST THE TOPICS YOU NEED TO REVISIT HERE.
INCLUDE RELEVANT PAGE NUMBERS AND/OR POWERPOINT LOCATIONS

Topic:

Topic:

Topic:

The Course Key

Unit Exam 2

EXAM SUMMARY:

FILL OUT THIS WORKSHEET IMMEDIATELY AFTER

THE TEST TO HELP PREPARE FOR THE FINAL

Question Themes:
List below all of the major themes you were not prepared for and prioritize them for the final exam.

Question Types:
Recall all question types used and to what frequency. Reflect on what types you need to practice.

Successes:
Recall topics you had good understanding of and could easily answer. When studying for the final exam, briefly review these topics and move on!

Unit Exam 3

REVIEW YOUR LECTURE NOTES, AND LIST THE TOPICS YOU NEED TO REVISIT HERE.
INCLUDE RELEVANT PAGE NUMBERS AND/OR POWERPOINT LOCATIONS

Topic:

Topic:

Topic:

The Course Key

Unit Exam 3

REVIEW YOUR LECTURE NOTES, AND LIST THE TOPICS YOU NEED TO REVISIT HERE.
INCLUDE RELEVANT PAGE NUMBERS AND/OR POWERPOINT LOCATIONS

Topic:

Topic:

Topic:

The Course Key

Unit Exam 3

REVIEW YOUR LECTURE NOTES, AND LIST THE TOPICS YOU NEED TO REVISIT HERE.
INCLUDE RELEVANT PAGE NUMBERS AND/OR POWERPOINT LOCATIONS

Topic:

Topic:

Topic:

The Course Key

Unit Exam 3

EXAM SUMMARY:

FILL OUT THIS WORKSHEET IMMEDIATELY AFTER

THE TEST TO HELP PREPARE FOR THE FINAL

Question Themes:
List below all of the major themes you were not prepared for and prioritize them for the final exam.

Question Types:
Recall all question types used and to what frequency. Reflect on what types you need to practice.

Successes:
Recall topics you had good understanding of and could easily answer. When studying for the final exam, briefly review these topics and move on!

The Course Key

Unit Exam 4

REVIEW YOUR LECTURE NOTES, AND LIST THE TOPICS YOU NEED TO REVISIT HERE.
INCLUDE RELEVANT PAGE NUMBERS AND/OR POWERPOINT LOCATIONS

Topic:

Topic:

Topic:

Unit Exam 4

REVIEW YOUR LECTURE NOTES, AND LIST THE TOPICS YOU NEED TO REVISIT HERE.
INCLUDE RELEVANT PAGE NUMBERS AND/OR POWERPOINT LOCATIONS

Topic:

Topic:

Topic:

The Course Key

Unit Exam 4

REVIEW YOUR LECTURE NOTES, AND LIST THE TOPICS YOU NEED TO REVISIT HERE.
INCLUDE RELEVANT PAGE NUMBERS AND/OR POWERPOINT LOCATIONS

Topic:

Topic:

Topic:

The Course Key

Unit Exam 4

EXAM SUMMARY:

FILL OUT THIS WORKSHEET IMMEDIATELY AFTER

THE TEST TO HELP PREPARE FOR THE FINAL

Question Themes:
List below all of the major themes you were not prepared for and prioritize them for the final exam.

Question Types:
Recall all question types used and to what frequency. Reflect on what types you need to practice.

Successes:
Recall topics you had good understanding of and could easily answer. When studying for the final exam, briefly review these topics and move on!

Final Exam

REVIEW YOUR UNIT EXAM NOTES, AND LIST THE TOPICS YOU NEED TO REVISIT HERE. INCLUDE RELEVANT PAGE NUMBERS AND/OR POWERPOINT LOCATIONS

Topic:

Topic:

Topic:

The Course Key

Final Exam

REVIEW YOUR UNIT EXAM NOTES, AND LIST THE TOPICS YOU NEED TO REVISIT HERE. INCLUDE RELEVANT PAGE NUMBERS AND/OR POWERPOINT LOCATIONS

Topic:

Topic:

Topic:

www.ingramcontent.com/pod-product-compliance
Lightning Source LLC
LaVergne TN
LVHW061312060426
835507LV00019B/2116